The Book on FMLA:

What It Is and How to Prevent Abuse
A handbook for Human Resources professionals

Steven Johnson,
MBA, PHR, SHRM-CP

Steven Cole Johnson, LLC
Indianapolis, Indiana

Copyright © 2015, 2016, 2019 by Steven Johnson. All rights reserved.

No part of this book may be reproduced in any form whatsoever, by photography or xerography or by another means, by broadcast of transmission, by translation into any kind of language, nor by recording electronically or otherwise, nor stored in a retrieval system, without permission in writing from the author, except by a reviewer, who may quote brief passages in articles or reviews.

ISBN 978-1-61422-906-3

Second printing December 2016

Paperback editions of this book are printed in the United States of America by CreateSpace.

Audio edition of this book is available on Audible.

For information, contact the author:
    Steven Johnson, MBA, PHR, SHRM-CP
    Steven.Johnson70@gmail.com
    StevenColeJohnson.com
    LinkedIn.com/in/StevenJohnson1

Acknowledgments and Dedication

My immeasurable thanks go to Rick Blacklidge for all your support, to Rosemary Robertson for editorial review, to Darren and all my colleagues at HHC/MCPHD for helping me discover the passion to serve and pushing me to succeed, to Serendipity, and to my parents – all four of them.

This book is dedicated to all of you.

Notice

This book is intended to provide general information and is not intended as legal advice. Please consult legal counsel.

Web site

Visit my Web site at www.StevenColeJohnson.com for contact information about training or speaking engagements.

Table of Contents

OBJECTIVES 1
FMLA: WHAT IS IT? 2
COVERED EMPLOYERS 3
ELIGIBLE EMPLOYEES 4
QUALIFYING EVENTS 6
FAMILY RELATIONSHIPS 8
EMPLOYER & EMPLOYEE NOTICES 10
CERTIFICATION 13
SERIOUS HEALTH CONDITION (SHC) 16
SHORT-TERM CONDITIONS 19
HEALTH CARE PROVIDER (HCP) 20
DEVELOP A PROCESS FOR MANAGING FMLA ... 21
PREVENT MISUSE 23
COMBAT (SUSPECTED) ABUSE 31
TRAIN YOUR MANAGERS 38
APPENDIX A: MANAGER TRAINING 42
APPENDIX B: TIMELINES AND DEADLINES 44
APPENDIX C: SAMPLE TEXT 45
CONCLUSION 47
ABOUT THE AUTHOR 49

Objectives

With this book, I want to help you learn about the Family and Medical Leave Act (FMLA) and to be more comfortable working with it, help you comply with the law, help your employees benefit from it, and help you guide your managers work with employees in using it.

Learn what FMLA is

FMLA is job-protected leave for certain family and medical reasons. We'll review covered employers and eligible employees, why an employee might need FMLA, and how best to manage it. I will then focus on helping you develop a process to manage it, which works towards preventing misuse. Finally, if you suspect abuse, I'll provide some ideas that can combat that.

Understand more how to manage FMLA

In my experience, not knowing enough about FMLA leads to confusion and anxiety for employees, for managers, and even for Human Resources. FMLA is for employees to take time off without fear of retribution or disciplinary action. Most people who use FMLA need it for a legitimate reason.

Prevent misuse and/or combat suspected abuse

I hope you can use this information to create your own action items, so you have steps you can take to apply it correctly, educate employees, prevent misuse, and/or stop FMLA abuse.

FMLA: What is it?

Job-protected leave
The Family and Medical Leave Act provides protection when taking time off work. The focus of this book is the federal FMLA, but you may also be subject to state or local leave laws.

The amount of time off
FMLA provides up to 12 workweeks of leave in a 12-month period; up to 26 workweeks of leave for military caregiver purposes. The 12-month period is discussed later in this book.

Unpaid time off
The regulations provide protection of time off but don't require paying the employee, so the leave itself is unpaid. It's up to the employer and/or the employee to decide whether sick time or some other block of paid time off is concurrent with FMLA.

Group health benefits continue
Employees' group health benefits in the employer's plan must continue as if they are working. The employee may pay the premiums due while on leave or the employer may elect to recover those costs once the employee returns to work.

Covered Employers

Private sector company conducting business

A person or organization involved in business or commerce with at least 50 employees, working 20 or more weeks each working year, within 75 miles of the employee's work site, is subject to the federal law.

Public agencies, educational agencies, & private schools

Public agencies (such as the federal, state, and local governments), educational agencies, & private schools are also covered, but the 50-employee & 50-employee-within-75-miles thresholds do not apply.

Eligible Employees

Under FMLA, "employee" and "hours worked" are defined generally as the same as under the Fair Labor Standards Act (FLSA).

Employee

Workers who are engaged in interstate commerce, production of goods for commerce, a closely-related process or occupation directly essential to such production, or domestic service are by and large considered employees by the Fair Labor Standards Act. Interstate commerce includes making telephone calls to or typing letters to send to other states, processing credit card applications, or traveling to other states. This definition is in addition to workers of an enterprise having at least two employees and whose annual gross volume of sales made or business done is not less than $500,000. Workers are employees also if the enterprise is engaged in the operation of a hospital, an institution primarily engaged in the care of the sick, the aged, or the mentally ill who reside on the premises; a school for mentally or physically disabled or gifted children; a preschool, an elementary or secondary school, or an institution of higher education (whether operated for profit or not for profit) or the common business purpose of the enterprise is an activity of a public agency.

Hours worked

"Hours worked" in general includes the time an employee must be on duty during the workday. Also included is any additional time the employee is allowed (i.e., suffered or permitted) to work.

Worked at least 12 months & at least 1,250 hours

To be eligible for FMLA, employees must have worked for the employer for at least 12 months and have worked at least 1,250 hours within the previous 12 months before their leave begins. The 12 months of employment do not have to be consecutive; a break in service doesn't automatically cause the 12-month period to start over. An employee may reach the threshold of hours worked before the 12 months has occurred.

Work within 75 miles of work site

Employees who work within 75 miles of their work site are eligible, if at least 50 employees work at that work site. This is measured as miles traveled on roads, not as the crow flies.

Qualifying Events

What's covered by FMLA? These events are called qualifying events.

Birth, adoption, foster care of a child

First, bringing a child into your family – the birth of a son or daughter and care of the newborn child; adoption or foster care placement of a child is also covered.

Care of the employee's spouse, child, or parent with a serious health condition

Second, the care of the employee's spouse, son, daughter, or parent with a serious health condition is covered. Defining family members and serious health conditions is discussed later in this book.

The employee's own serious health condition

Third, the employee's own serious health condition is covered.

Military exigency resulting from military duty of the employee's spouse, child, or parent

Fourth, FMLA is also for a military exigency or requirement coming from the employee's spouse's, son's, daughter's, or parent's active duty or federal call to active duty. A military exigency is for activities related to the active duty, and includes deployment ceremonies and programs, child care and school activities, making financial and legal arrangements, rest, and recuperation when the military member is given short-term leave, and post-deployment activities like an arrival ceremony.

Care for a covered service member with a serious injury or illness

Fifth, military caregiver leave provides up to 26 workweeks for care of a covered service member with a serious injury or illness that occurred in the line of duty or was aggravated by service in the line of duty.

Family Relationships

I don't want to tell you your family business, but here's what the FMLA says about it.

Child (Son or Daughter)

A son or daughter is your biological, adopted, or foster child, or stepchild, or legal ward, or a child of a person standing in loco parentis (more on that term in a moment). The son or daughter must be under 18 years of age, or 18 or older and incapable of self-care due to a mental or physical disability. Being incapable of self-care means the person is unable to provide 3 or more activities of daily living (ADLs) for himself/herself, and that's an important element.

Parent

A parent is the biological, adoptive, step-, or foster care mother or father. It's also someone who stands or stood in loco parentis when the employee was under the age of 18 or incapable of self-care.

The term in loco parentis means that person who has or had responsibilities on a day-to-day basis for the child. This could be unmarried, second parent relationships, grandparents or another relative if they raised the child, and legal guardians.

Spouse

Who can marry may have changed, but until 2015, the definition of spouse for FMLA was a husband or wife as recognized under the state law in the state where the employee resides. In February 2015, the Department of

Labor issued a final rule to recognize marriages based on place of celebration. The rule became effective March 27, 2015 and ensures that all married couples are treated equally under FMLA. Furthermore, in the 2015 Obergefell v. Hodges case, the U.S. Supreme Court held that marriage is a fundamental right and legal for same-sex couples.

Next of Kin

For purposes of FMLA and a covered service member, next of kin is the nearest blood relative other than that service member's spouse, parent, son, or daughter. This may be someone designated by the service member or not. A covered service member is a member of the armed forces who is receiving treatment or care for a serious injury or illness. Also included is a veteran receiving treatment or care for a serious injury or illness and who was a member of the armed forces during the period of five years preceding the beginning of that treatment or care.

Employer & Employee Notices

Employer Notice

Employers are required by federal law to post in conspicuous places a notice explaining the FMLA provisions.

WH-1420 Employee Rights and Responsibilities

You can meet the requirements of federal law by posting the WH-1420, the Department of Labor handout titled Employee Rights and Responsibilities. In addition, you may distribute it to all employees or provide the equivalent information in your handbook. You may also provide this information via employer-provided electronic communication systems.

WH-381 Notice of Eligibility and Rights & Responsibilities

WH-381 is the Department of Labor's Notice of Eligibility and Rights & Responsibilities that you can use to notify employees of their eligibility to take leave under FMLA.

WH-382 Designation Notice

WH-382 is the Department of Labor's Designation Notice, and you can use this to give written designation that the employee's leave qualifies for FMLA.

The Department of Labor does not require use of their prototype forms. You can adapt them as needed, as long as you don't ask for information prohibited by FMLA. Take action if you are not currently using these forms or their equivalents: implement use of these forms because they are extremely useful.

Employee Notice

If an employee knows he/she needs to take leave, meaning it's a foreseeable need for time off, at least 30 days' notice is required or as soon as practicable, absent unusual circumstances. For example, an employee who is requesting time off for bonding with a new baby generally would know that they need time off at least 30 days beforehand. Notice of less than 30 days is possible even with a foreseeable need, such as having surgery or receiving treatment on an urgent basis. This is where managers can help Human Resources' administration of FMLA. The manager may need to remind employees to request FMLA information from Human Resources.

If the leave is unforeseeable, employees need to give notice as soon as practicable, or capable of being done. An example of this is an employee who is injured or gets ill and needs time off for treatment, surgery, recovery, etc. Employees need to give notice of time off according to your regular procedures, whether that's calling a specific telephone number, or notifying his/her immediate supervisor.

Recognize an employee's need for FMLA

It's important for Human Resources professionals and managers to recognize an employee's need for FMLA. An employee's comments about his or her medical condition or impending absences may invoke the protections of FMLA, even if the employee does not specifically mention FMLA. The amount of time off required by a health care provider, the number of treatments or appointments for the condition, or a medication prescription may result in an FMLA-covered condition. When known, the manager or Human Resources professional may have an obligation to remind the employee of the availability of FMLA.

Certification

When an employee claims the need for FMLA, are you going to take his/her word for it, or do you want independent verification?

Employer can require the employee's leave be supported by certification

Employees can be required to provide certification to support the need for time off. The requirement applies to the employee's own serious health condition, or that of the employee's spouse, child, or parent, as well as qualifying exigencies and caregiver leave for a covered service member. Legal documentation may be required in the case of adoption or foster care. The WH-381 Notice of Eligibility and Rights & Responsibilities notifies employees of the requirement to provide certification.

DOL prototype forms

Again, the DOL provides prototype forms for certification. Employers can develop their own forms for certification, but those may not ask for more information than the certification asks for.

Provides medical facts, symptoms, diagnosis, Rx, regimen of treatment

The medical certifications ask for medical facts sufficient to support the need for time off. This may include the patient's symptoms or diagnosis, prescriptions, regimen of treatment, and hospitalization.

Provides information on the inability to perform essential duties

The employee certification also asks for why the employee can't perform his/her duties; the family member certification asks for why the family member is in need of care.

Frequency & duration

Certification is essential so the health care provider can tell you, the employer, why it is medically necessary to take the leave. If a serious health condition causes flare-ups that could prevent the employee from coming to work, the health care provider needs to provide an estimate of the frequency and duration of flare-ups.

Require the forms to be complete and sufficient

Employers may require the certification forms to be complete, meaning not having one or more blanks, and be sufficiently answered, meaning answers cannot be vague or confusing. Without all of the questions answered and understandable, evaluating the medical need for time off is more difficult.

Contact with health care provider (HCP)

The employer may contact the health care provider when the certification is complete and sufficient only to authenticate and clarify the certification. This is to verify that the information was provided or authorized by the health care provider, and to understand the handwriting or the meaning of what's written on the certification. Employers may not ask for more information than what is required by the certification.

Contact with the health care provider is by the Human Resources staff, a management official, or the employer's own health care provider. Employers may establish procedures designating the official contact person.

The employee's immediate supervisor may not contact the health care provider regarding FMLA.

This requirement can apply to the initial certification, annual certifications for conditions lasting beyond a single leave year, and the recertification when sending the employee back to the health care provider.

On forms you already accepted, you may not be able to go back and require them to be complete, but you can require completeness going forward. If you have been working from incomplete or vague certifications, give yourself an action item to change this going forward.

Serious Health Condition (SHC)

Illness, injury, impairment, or physical or mental condition, inpatient care

A serious health condition could be an illness, injury, impairment, or some condition where the patient is admitted for an overnight stay or where the patient is receiving continuing treatment. Due to the serious health condition, the patient is unable to work or perform regular activities of daily living (ADLs).

Incapacity is the inability to work or perform regular daily activities

Let's say an employee goes to the emergency room and is admitted overnight, causing incapacity. During that time, the health care provider likely is performing tests to evaluate the condition and may be beginning a course of medications. After a couple nights in the hospital, the employee is sent home with orders to rest for a few more days before going back to work. The employee is then to return to the health care provider in a couple of weeks for follow-up tests. Using this information, the employee almost certainly has a serious health condition that qualifies under FMLA. This is due to having been admitted for an overnight stay and receiving a regimen of treatment.

Treatment includes exams to determine if a SHC exists and evaluations of it

Treatment also includes the exams to determine if a serious health condition exists and to evaluate the condition. This may involve a situation where the employee and his/her health care provider know something is going on but it hasn't been completely diagnosed or a regimen for continuing treatment has not been started.

Continuing treatment

During the period of incapacity, receiving treatment at least two or more times by a health care provider within the first thirty days of incapacity is necessary. Furthermore, treatment on at least one of those occasions results in a regimen of continuing treatment supervised by the health care provider. Continuing treatment includes a period of incapacity or the inability to work due to pregnancy or prenatal care.

Chronic serious health condition

A chronic condition is one that exists for an extended length of time and could have instances that cause an absence. Examples include asthma, migraines, even cancer because of regular appointments, treatments, or flare-ups. Chronic conditions may create episodic absences and not always be an incapacity that occurs only once.

Permanent/long-term

A permanent or long-term condition differs from chronic, in that a patient is under the supervision of a health care provider but ongoing treatment is not effective. This is when the condition exists but the patient isn't actively receiving treatment, such as having suffered an acute stroke or is in the terminal stages of a disease.

Substance abuse as a serious health condition

Receiving treatment for substance abuse, if all requirements of treatment of a serious health condition are met, may be a serious health condition under FMLA. Notice that is receiving treatment for substance abuse. This does not mean an employee's absence due to having used the substance is covered by FMLA. FMLA does not protect the employee from disciplinary action for substance use or abuse, but does protect the employee during absences for treatment.

Short-term Conditions

Cold, flu, dental appointments, routine exams

By themselves, conditions lasting only a short time are not serious health conditions under FMLA. These are conditions that require only a brief treatment and recovery plan. However, if an employee experiences complications or if the condition causes additional time off or includes an ongoing regimen of treatment, this may result in an FMLA-qualified serious health condition.

Health Care Provider (HCP)

Health care provider

A health care provider is any person determined by the U.S. Secretary of Labor as capable of providing health care services. The list includes but is not limited to the following:

- Doctor of Medicine, Doctor of Osteopathy,
- Podiatrists, Dentists, Chiropractors,
- Nurse Practitioners, Physician's Assistants,
- Nurse-midwives, Clinical Social Workers, Psychologists,
- Christian Science practitioners, and
- One of these, outside the U.S., authorized by a country to practice in that country

Develop a Process for Managing FMLA

How are you currently managing FMLA? Is it working for you, your employees, and your managers? Do your employees know how to request FMLA? Do employees know and follow the process? Are all employees held to the same standard?

Employees should contact Human Resources regarding need for time off

Your process for managing FMLA should involve educating your employees, including informing them to contact Human Resources when they need time off for medical or personal situations. This may be including FMLA training in programs such as New Employee Orientation.

Stating "FMLA" not required

Employees don't have to reference FMLA in order to invoke the protections of the law; this means they don't have to know the terminology. They simply have to indicate the need for time off because of an event that could qualify for FMLA. What's important is to have employees come to Human Resources and not request FMLA from their manager. Your procedure should be to provide forms directly to employees or their family members, not giving forms to employees' managers or other employees. Doing this helps ensure there is separation between FMLA and the employee's manager.

Require proper use of forms

Your process should also include requiring forms to be complete and on time. When you hand over the forms, you have an opportunity to inform employees when the forms are to be returned and that every question must be answered.

Having a process establishes consistency

Putting a process in place communicates consistency on your part and can help prevent or refute claims of discrimination. Consistency is the key to all policies, procedures, practices, and processes.

Making changes

Employers may change their process for administering FMLA. Any changes must be formally announced to managers and employees. Otherwise, the employer who fails to properly announce policy changes could be held liable for inconsistent, unfair, or biased FMLA practices.

Prevent Misuse

Some of the following information refers back to the employer and employee notice requirements, as well as developing, improving, or reinforcing your process. Much of this section can also serve as notice to employees that you monitor their use of FMLA and take steps to ensure they're using FMLA properly.

Documentation must be complete and sufficient

As part of your process, you can require that request forms and certifications are complete, meaning every question must be completed; every field must have a response, or a "not applicable" to indicate it has not been neglected. Answers must also not be vague, or be simply "as needed," "unknown," or "to be determined." You may need to proceed on good faith sometimes and work with the employee to determine the need for time off while taking steps to fulfill your requirements. This shows compassion during an employee's medical or personal situation, and still tells this employee and others that you hold everyone to the same standard. As you know, employees talk to each other about their interaction with Human Resources. Simply enforcing this requirement can go a long way towards preventing misuse or abuse, because the certification is your source of information about the employee's condition and how it affects his/her attendance. I cannot stress enough the importance of having complete and understandable documentation.

Contact health care provider when needed

Employers may contact the health care provider – not to get more than what the certification asks for – but to authenticate the certification or to clarify responses provided.

Authentication

You may need to authenticate or confirm that the information provided came from or was authorized by the health care provider. Take for example, a nurse or other employee in the health care provider's office completes the form, and then the doctor just signs it. Or, the doctor's employee answers some of the questions and leaves the rest for the doctor to complete. You could have a certification with two (or more) types of handwriting or some answers written in blue ink and others in black ink. Did your employee fill out the doctor's certification? Did your employee add these responses after the doctor signed it? You may need to authenticate this certification.

Clarification

If you don't understand the handwriting or the meaning of something in the certification, you need to seek clarification. This has to be done just so you can evaluate the need for time off.

Limit who may contact the health care provider

At no time is the employee's immediate supervisor contacting the health care provider. Human Resources or, if established by company procedures, senior management can be in communication with the health care provider. You're not using this opportunity to ask the health care provider if the employee really needs time off. Contacting the health care provider is to help you understand what is presented on the certification.

Require concurrent use of paid time off

If you offer any type of paid time off for employees, it is strongly recommended that you make them use it at the same time as FMLA. This includes using sick time, vacation, combined PTO, or whatever you call it, while on leave. By requiring concurrent use of paid time off, an employee is prevented from stacking unpaid FMLA days off with other sick or vacation days, or saving paid time off for future use. Not all employees would think of saving up their paid hours simply to extend their time off, but some may.

Delay use of FMLA when necessary

Another method to prevent misuse of FMLA is to delay an employee's time off. This is going to apply to consecutive use of FMLA, and you're really only able to request an employee delay his/her time off because the documentation is incomplete or the employee has failed to follow the notice requirements.

Be aware that any delay could impact the treatment plan to help the employee. My advice is to act carefully. The better you inform your employees of the requirements, the better you'll be able to enforce them. Whenever an employee fails to provide certification from the health care provider, you could delay use of FMLA because without the certification, you may be unable to confirm how much time off is necessary. However, in the case of an emergency health care issue, you may receive information piece-meal from an authorized family member or health care provider and will have to use your best judgment. For example, you may need to proceed on good faith in the event an employee is in a coma or has experienced an aneurysm. You may choose to proceed with partial or piece-meal information until the employee is able to participate in the process.

The 12-month period

Except in the case of leave to care for a covered service member, the regulations allow employers to choose from 4 different methods to calculate the 12-month period in which employees may take leave.

The first method is to use the calendar year, beginning on January 1st and ending on December 31st. This means a new 12-month period begins every January 1st. An employee could use the last 12 weeks of one year, and the first 12 weeks of the next year – essentially taking off for a consecutive 24 weeks.

The second method is any fixed 12-month period, such as your fiscal year, the employee's anniversary date, or any other year. This method allows stacking leaves in the same manner as the calendar year.

The third method is called "look forward," which does not take into account how much FMLA has been used previously. This is 12 weeks of leave beginning on the first date FMLA leave is taken, and is the only method to be used for military caregiver leave.

The fourth, and recommended, method is the rolling year or "look back." In this method, the 12 weeks of leave are measured looking backward from the first date the employee uses leave. The amount of leave an employee has available is the balance of the 12 weeks not used in the past 12-month period. This is the method that eliminates the possibility of stacking leaves from one year to the next, because an employee has only the hours remaining that have not been used in the past 12 months.

You may be able to change from one method to another, by providing employees with at least 60 days' notice. Employees whose leave falls within the transition period must receive the greater benefit method, which means you cannot end their FMLA benefit early or reduce their already-approved FMLA time off.

Require annual certification

For employees who use FMLA for chronic or long-term conditions, employers should require annual certifications. Quite simply, the employee's condition may change over time, so to have a new certification each year informs you easily of any changes in that employee's condition or how his/her attendance could be affected. Whether you choose to notify employees when they reach the end of their FMLA period or adopt a wait-and-see concept is up to you. You could also remind the employee's manager as the end of the 12-month period approaches. Ultimately, you may save yourself some time and aggravation by notifying the employee directly and preemptively sending a new request form and certification. Requiring annual certification provides employers with the same opportunity to authenticate and clarify the certifications and these certifications are subject to second and third opinions if necessary.

Require checking in before returning from consecutive leave

When employees are on leave for a consecutive period, have them check in prior to their return. Not only are you helping prepare for their return by notifying their managers, you're also confirming they have an intention to return. How and when you choose to have them check in is up to you. One possibility is just a phone call, such as two weeks before the end of their leave or check in during week four and again during week eight. Having them check in with you helps maintain the FMLA-based relationship employees have with Human Resources.

Require return-to-work release

The check-in is also when you can remind employees they must have a return-to-work statement from their health care provider. Requiring this statement prevents the employee from trying to return early or to extend his/her time off without the health care provider's knowledge.

Include a personal leave of absence in policy

Include some kind of personal leave into your policy, if you don't have one already. This allows you to grant additional time off, without having to call it FMLA. I know, you're now asking how giving more time off will help prevent employees from taking advantage of you. If you let employees take more than 12 work weeks and call it FMLA, you could be starting a dangerous precedent. If you terminate an employee immediately upon exhausting his/her available FMLA time, that could also be a dangerous precedent. You may not want to have to terminate because you could be losing a great employee, but that employee is just not able to return to work yet. By having another kind of leave, whatever you call it, with or without the same protections of FMLA, you are better able to balance the employer's needs with the employee's needs. A personal leave may also be used as an accommodation under the Americans with Disabilities Act, and you're using this time to continue the dialog with the employee in evaluating work available for that returning employee.

Prohibit employees from working 2nd jobs while using time off under any leave

Why would an employer be concerned about employees working second jobs? Suppose one of your employees works part-time in retail. Then, around the end of the year, that employee is claiming FMLA and taking time off work. But when you go shopping on your lunch break to take advantage of special sale prices that day, you see that employee working as a cashier. If the FMLA certification states the employee can't do any of his/her work functions, you may have a case of FMLA fraud. By prohibiting employees upfront from working any job while claiming time off under FMLA, you are informing the employee that you know FMLA is for the inability to work at all. An employee may challenge this stipulation, so a well-developed job description allows that employee's health care provider to advise what work the employee cannot do for your employer but still may be able to perform the functions of the second job.

Communicate FMLA policy & expectations to employees and managers

Be sure to communicate your FMLA policy to your employees. This may be as simple as posting the FMLA notice in Human Resources or some other prominent location, or including it in your policy handbook. You may choose to review FMLA during New Employee Orientation or in some other training. What you include is up to you, but at the very least, I recommend providing all employees with the information contained in the WH-1420 Employee Rights and Responsibilities Under the Family and Medical Leave Act. Your employee training may also explain that complete documentation is required, that approval for time off may be delayed, or that employees could be transferred to a different position when regular, planned absences occur during their use of FMLA.

It's important also to communicate why FMLA is being used and under what conditions an employee may call off work. In your approval, you're informing the employee and his/her manager how much time off the employee needs. Repeat what is on the certification regarding whether an employee is using FMLA for appointments only or for episodic flare-ups also. For example, "The health care provider has stated that flare-ups could occur up to two times per month with a duration of up to two days per episode." The approval can also be used to inform employees that they must use the correct call-off procedure regarding FMLA.

Combat (Suspected) Abuse

What can you do if you suspect an employee is misusing or abusing FMLA? This generally applies more closely to intermittent use of FMLA because it has a greater potential for misuse and abuse.

Have consistency on your side

Because you have an established process that you have communicated to all employees, you have consistency on your side.

Review attendance

The first thing you're going to do is to review the employee's attendance and compare that with the information presented on the certification. Is there a pattern of use? Suppose an employee claims FMLA, and it just happens to always be the Monday following your football team's home games. Or the employee consistently claims FMLA on the third Thursday of the month, which happens to be the day he or she is assigned to work on a particular task. Also, is the employee using more time off than anticipated? If an employee exceeds his/her time off on a consistent basis, this could be one employee to review regularly.

What FMLA is used for

Is the employee claiming FMLA for appointments or flare-ups? Not all conditions have flare-ups. If an employee is saying his/her condition is having a flare-up, Human Resources and the employee's manager should already know whether flare-ups are included in the use of FMLA because that was included in the certification. Frequency and duration of flare-ups may equal a lot of time off each week or month, so monitor total time off.

Get a 2nd (or 3rd) opinion on certification

If you have reason to doubt the validity of a certification, you may require the employee to get a second or third opinion. These are at the employer's expense. While you're sending the employee for a second opinion, he/she is entitled provisionally to the benefits of the act. So, act on good faith for the employee and seek to confirm the need really exists.

The second health care provider is not employed by you on a regular basis. Your employee is entitled to reimbursement for travel expenses and may not be required to travel outside the normal commuting area. If the second opinion differs from the certification of the first health care provider, you may need to send the employee for a third opinion, which is binding on both the employee and employer.

Send employee for recertification

Another method to combat abuse if you suspect it, is to send the employee back to his/her health care provider for recertification. This may be used to confirm or update the initial certification, and is different from the annual certification for chronic or long-term conditions. (In the section on preventing misuse, I recommended requiring employees using FMLA beyond a single leave year to obtain certification every year. If you're not doing that already, this is your call to action.)

Sending an employee for recertification may be necessary if the use of FMLA changes or if the employer gets information that casts doubt on the employee's reason for the absence. An employee's use of FMLA may be for doctor appointments only if the certification indicated the condition will not cause episodic flare-ups. However, twice last month and once so far this month, an employee calls off work claiming FMLA. You remember that when you issued FMLA approval, the employee questioned why it was for doctor appointments only. The type of absence has changed from what the health care provider indicated on the certification. Sending the employee back to the health care provider allows for an update within the FMLA period. This shows compassion for your employee because it's possibly expanding the use of FMLA to further protect absences. It also signals that you review employees' use of FMLA to maintain compliance. In this example, an updated certification may now indicate flare-ups could occur. Or, nothing changes and you can remind the employee that according to the health care provider the FMLA is only for appointments.

An employee's manager may learn that an employee who took leave, claiming FMLA, was actually working a second job or doing something inconsistent with his/her need for FMLA. For example, an employee is using FMLA for severe back pain and calls off work but later posts a picture that day on social media of himself riding an all-terrain vehicle. Apparently his pain was so bad that he couldn't work, but he was still able to ride the ATV. As the Human Resources administrator, you will need to compare his reason for FMLA with what he's actually doing. A conversation with the employee may clarify what he was doing or may prevent future abuse. With this example, try to determine if he was riding the ATV that day instead of being at work, or if the picture was taken another day.

Include job description and attendance record

When you send the employee for recertification, include his/her job description and a copy of his/her attendance record with a copy of the initial certification. You then instruct the employee to take this documentation to his/her health care provider and get a statement from the health care provider regarding whether the need for the FMLA leave continues, whether there has been any change in the medical facts prompting the need for FMLA, and what the anticipated length and frequency of time off will be, if time is needed.

Recertification is at the employee's expense, and that factor alone could curb abuse if it's occurring. You're now telling employees you review their use of FMLA and suspicion of abuse could cost them. Employees may have to utilize their paid time off to go back to the health care provider, may have to pay a co-pay at the doctor's office, and may have to pay to have the certification reviewed and updated.

In my experience, recertification has been effective in reducing suspected abuse.

Use surveillance

You can also use surveillance to investigate and stop suspected abuse of FMLA. Let me be clear about this: the employee's supervisor is not performing the surveillance. But the supervisor may hear from other employees about someone's use of FMLA. Employees having to fill in for an absent employee may be reporting that they have learned what the employee is really doing on his/her time off.

Someone in Human Resources trained in investigations may be an option. Or, if you have professional security employees, such as those who are deputized by your police or sheriff's department, they're likely trained to conduct investigations. Otherwise, use an outside private investigator to observe the employee suspected of abusing FMLA. What you need is for that person to follow and video record what your employee is doing while claiming the inability to work. You can then show the video to your employee. It may be that the employee is working a second job, or riding that ATV on the day he claimed time off under FMLA.

Surveillance can be costly, especially if you are using a private investigator because that is possibly going to go on for several days or longer. You may determine the investment is worthwhile. This may be the only option if you're not using the rolling (look-back) 12-month period and you cannot change the 12-month period currently in place and you suspect than an employee is claiming FMLA fraudulently.

Terminate for known abuse of FMLA

An extreme measure to combat abuse is to terminate the employee for fraudulent use of FMLA. After taking steps to confirm legitimate uses of FMLA, trying everything else to get the employee to do his/her job, and finding that an employee is deceptively using FMLA, you may choose to terminate his/her employment.

Have a conversation with the employee, to notify him/her that you have evidence that works in your favor. Then, decide if you're going to terminate or not. As with any disciplinary action, what you hold back from today, you may be revisiting again in the future.

The action you take sends the message to all of your employees of whether you permit abuse of FMLA or not. Another note about this option: You haven't disciplined or retaliated against the employee for using FMLA; your action is because the employee has claimed FMLA fraudulently.

Permit employee to exhaust available FMLA hours

Your administration of FMLA may also include simply letting employees exhaust their available hours. Letting them run out of FMLA hours may force the employee to decide on a course of action such as changing to part-time or changing jobs altogether. I'm not without compassion and I don't want to sound completely heartless. Employees with challenging health conditions need FMLA for legitimate reasons. But it's Human Resources' and management's responsibility to balance taking care of the employee and making sure your company can do its job.

Use disciplinary action for performance-based problems and/or policy violations

An employee using FMLA is not free from disciplinary action due to poor work performance or policy violations. Use your progressive discipline structure to correct employees' productivity problems. That may be news to some; it may be obvious to others. I had a conversation with a manager who felt she could not discipline a low-performing employee because the employee was using FMLA on an intermittent basis. When the employee is not using FMLA, meaning that employee is at work, his/her work performance has certain expectations. Because FMLA is administered by Human Resources and work performance is managed by the employee's chain of command, these issues are separated from each other. Just be aware, Human Resources and management must be able to defend the action taken.

Disciplinary action that's focused on when the employee is at work must be well-documented. While moving through your progressive discipline structure, from a verbal reprimand to a written reprimand, and possibly to a final warning or termination of employment, you must be able to defend your actions of trying to get the employee to improve his/her work output. And you haven't mentioned FMLA.

Train Your Managers

I love the conversations with the managers I support. They tell me the greatest stories about their employees, what employees say when calling in, and how they're ready to jump off the roof because of how fun – uh, I mean – how frustrating being a manager is.

I realized after having the same conversation with multiple managers, they need my help. (I also realized how great it felt to be needed, but that's a topic for another book.)

So I developed an FMLA training session to help them, which in turn helped me. Now cue the soft music and imagine a place where Human Resources and management works together...

Helps achieve consistency

By training managers on the FMLA policy, you can achieve consistency in the overall administration of it. This could be a big action item for you – put together a handout, a full-blown presentation, or something in between to tell managers your FMLA policy. Training your managers gives them the confidence to manage employees within the protections of FMLA.

Recognize the need for FMLA

Managers need to understand enough about FMLA to recognize when an employee might need it. An employee calls off work, saying "I'm sick today and can't leave the bathroom." That condition may or may not be FMLA-related because we don't know enough about it right now. But the employee who calls and says, "I've been sick all weekend and need to go see my doctor today" may be a little closer to a need for FMLA. Some employees share too much information and describe in detail more than you really want to know. I would give you an example of that, but you've probably heard enough from employees to understand my point.

Send employee to Human Resources for FMLA forms/questions

Managers need to listen for how long the employee has been sick, if he/she has been to a doctor or hospital and will have to go back for a follow-up, or if any medications have been prescribed. These are clues that the employee should contact Human Resources and request documentation for the time off. The employee doesn't have to say, "I need FMLA." Employees only have to indicate the need for time off, so employers may not use as a defense, "The employee didn't ask specifically for FMLA forms." The employee does not even have to be the one to request the documentation for FMLA; the request for leave can come from a family member or other responsible person.

Expectations for employee's attendance

Ensure your managers know the expectations for their employees' attendance when approved for FMLA. Generally, the approval should describe if FMLA is approved for consecutive blocks of time, or intermittently for appointments and episodic flare-ups.

For example, an employee may have appointments every 3 months which could take up to 4 hours for each appointment. Or, that employee has episodic flare-ups that could occur once a week with a duration of 1 day each episode. This information is taken from the health care provider's certification, and is important information to share with an employee's manager.

By sharing this information with the employee and his/her manager, you are communicating to the manager how the attendance of that employee could be affected. More importantly, you are telling the employee that his/her manager also knows how much time off is approved.

Another thing to train your managers on is that they need to tell their employees the procedure for calling off work. For appointments in advance, does the department require a paper leave slip or is an email message acceptable? For episodic flare-ups, are employees to call or text the manager's cell phone or a specific office number, then follow-up with the paper leave slip? When calling off work, employees are to reveal absences are related to their use of FMLA, in order to account for the employee's time properly. If an employee simply calls off "sick," that's not necessarily notifying their manager they are using FMLA and therefore are not eligible for the protections of FMLA. Managers can always ask whether a planned or unplanned absence is FMLA-related or not.

Monitor time off

The reason to tell managers how much time off an employee may need is not only so they can plan their workforce, but also so they can monitor the employee's use of FMLA. How many days each week or month an employee may be off work for FMLA then can be compared against the certification from the health care provider. Managers should continually monitor this to determine if a pattern emerges from their employee's use of FMLA. Does the use of FMLA coincide with a weekly assignment? Is it the same day of the week or month? What happened the day before or night before that causes an absence to occur the same day each week?

Contact Human Resources for next steps

Train your managers that if a pattern seems to emerge, they should contact Human Resources to review their employee's use of FMLA and advise next steps.

By working together, Human Resources and management can formulate a cohesive plan to address an employee's use or suspected abuse of FMLA and any performance-based issues that employee could be having. Again, the difficult task is balancing taking care of the employee and making sure your company can do its job. Human Resources can then take steps to ensure an employee is using FMLA properly and ensure the employer maintains compliance with the law.

Appendix A: Manager Training

The following suggestions may help you to develop a presentation to train your managers. Each of the headings represents a slide with the topics you can provide in your presentation.

Introduction to FMLA

What FMLA is, eligibility, qualifying events

Recognize the Need for FMLA

Listen for cues from employees about the number of days off work, the need for prescriptions, multiple appointments, or the inability to perform activities of daily living

Send Employees to Human Resources

This not only benefits Human Resources, but this can take the burden off managers

Approval and Use of FMLA

Informs management of an employee's approval for FMLA and what to expect for that employee's attendance

Communicate with Employees

Reinforce the method to be used by employees when requesting time off work for the FMLA-related reason

Monitor the Use of FMLA

Compare the actual time off to the expectations provided in the FMLA approval from Human Resources

Contact Human Resources

Bring suspicions, comparisons of time off with expectations, and questions to Human Resources

Appendix B: Timelines and Deadlines

This information highlights important timelines and deadlines from the regulation covering FMLA.

Employee Notice

At least 30 days' notice, if leave is foreseeable.
As soon as practicable, if leave is unforeseeable, or will be in less than 30 days.

Employee's Eligibility

Within five (5) business days of learning that an employee's absence may be FMLA-qualified, provide the employee of eligibility to take FMLA leave.

Certification

The employer must give an employee at least fifteen (15) calendar days to return certification to the employer.

Designation

Designation must be provided within five (5) business days after receiving enough information (i.e., certification) that an employee qualifies for FMLA leave.

Appendix C: Sample Text

These may help you to prepare your responses to requests for FMLA. Create a template or plain, unformatted document with text you will use frequently.

Approval and Usage

Your request for FMLA for your serious health condition is approved from [begin date] – [end date] on a consecutive basis.

This period may be shortened or extended based upon the health care provider's recommendation, a statement of which may be faxed to my attention at [insert telephone number].

Your request for FMLA for your child's serious health condition is approved on an intermittent basis from [begin date] – [end date].

The use of FMLA is for episodic flare-ups periodically preventing you from performing your job functions. Your health care provider has stated that flare-ups could occur up to X times per week/month with a duration of incapacity up to X hours/days per episode.

The use of FMLA is for appointments and episodic flare-ups periodically preventing your child in participating in normal daily activities, which require your care.

Appointments should be scheduled to minimize disruption to company operations, such as at the beginning or end of the work day or during anticipated slower periods of the work week.

You are to notify your management of appointments or absences according to the department's regular notification procedures and inform them that the absence is related to your use of FMLA.

Time Keeping

In [time-keeping], FSICK will be used first for available sick hours, then FVAC for available vacation hours, then FPTO for unpaid time off. Supervisors are responsible for monitoring the number of hours used.

Return to Work

I must have a return-to-work statement on or before your first day back to work and I will notify your management when I receive that.

Please check in with me [check-in period] prior to your return to work. I can be reached at [insert telephone number]. This is to confirm your return-to-work date.

I have received a statement that John Doe may return to full duty on [return date] with no restrictions.

Period Ending, Annual Certification

This use of FMLA will end on [end date] and the file will close automatically. A new certification is required to use FMLA after this date.

FMLA Not Available, Not Approved

Because you have not completed at least twelve months of employment or 1,250 hours of work preceding your request for FMLA, your request for FMLA cannot be approved at this time.

Your request for FMLA cannot be approved at this time. The certification submitted does not describe a health condition adequately to evaluate the need for time off.

Conclusion

I mentioned to a colleague at SHRM's Annual Conference in June 2014 that I would be submitting a presentation for the 2015 annual conference. When he asked about my topic, I casually answered, "FMLA, because it's a topic I enjoy." His response was, "Oh, you're the one!"

Yes, I'm the one who enjoys working with FMLA. And now I hope you will come to enjoy (or at least feel more comfortable) administering FMLA for your employer.

When I first began managing FMLA, I heard all sorts of horror stories. Then I discovered I liked helping the employees I support make proper use of it, I liked guiding the managers working with employees using it, and I obviously liked ensuring my employer was in compliance with the law.

I hope you have found this book helpful in learning about and managing FMLA for your employer. Also, I hope you identified some action steps that you can take to streamline your FMLA process and maybe even improve how you administer it.

I'd love to hear from you with questions or comments. Feel free to connect with me on LinkedIn or through my Web site at www.StevenColeJohnson.com

About the Author

My experience includes a variety of business responsibilities and all areas of Human Resources, with specific focus on compliance, employee relations, and training and development. I hold an MBA from Western Governors University and a bachelor's degree in theatre from Indiana State University. My experience ranges from human resource positions to directing and producing theatrical productions. Perhaps most surprisingly, the skills used to direct plays and musicals transfer very well to Human Resources. Training and advising on employee matters and corralling actors are remarkably comparable – following policies or following scripts, doing them the right way builds an efficient workforce and gets a standing ovation!

I live in Indianapolis, Indiana where I have been involved with many of the professional and community theatres, including being the founding director of Oaklandon Civic Theatre. One of my favorite productions is *The Christmas Quilt*, a play I wrote and directed that included popular Christmas songs. My involvement in theatre ranges from acting and directing, producing and designing to business management.

I am also involved in the Scottish Society of Indianapolis and the Indianapolis Scottish Highland Games and Festival. I am descended from the Douglas Clan through my maternal grandmother as well as other Scottish clans.

Made in United States
North Haven, CT
14 June 2023